Activities to do While You Number Two

An Adult Activity Book

Featuring 50 Adult Activities: Sudoku, Dot-to-Dot, Word Searches, Mazes, Fallen Phrases, Number Blocks, Word Tiles, Find the Shadow, Spot the Difference, Draw the Other Half, Nanograms, Brick-by-Brick, Word Scramble, and Much More!

Tamara L Adams

Each page has a fun adult activity.

Thank you for your purchase!
I hope you enjoy this book that is dedicated to
those who take a lot of time to poo!!

Please consider leaving a review and checking out my
Amazon collection!

Contact me to get a free printable PDF of activities at:
http://www.tamaraladamsauthor.com/free-printable-activity-book-pdf/

http://www.amazon.com/T.L.-Adams/e/B00YSROGC4

tamaraadamsauthor@gmail.com

www.tamaraladamsauthor.com

https://twitter.com/@TamaraLAdams

https://www.facebook.com/TamaraLAdamsAuthor/

https://www.pinterest.com/tamara-l-adams-author/

All Cartoon Drawings are from https://publicdomainvectors.org

Squeeze out this one: Connect the dots from 100 to 116 Don't let the extra numbers fool you!

230
218   258   278   240   276
268
124   233   233 248 264   245   244   243
242
223   246   249   105   238
238   246   125   104   106   237
254   243 245   247   237
253   119
257   121   255   272
251   254   279   255   274   239
265   226   120 275   236
270   254
271   248   166
230   127   249
262   264   168 167
258   185   236
238   250   259   169   265
256   241   257   272
242 269 239   212   243
241   247   266
259   239   214   210   269
244   123   171   170   241   267
253   262   239
239   222   195   260
237   268
237   236 259 226   261   172   250 245
236   256   263
268 225   196
211 239   277   271   174
235   197   236   263
212   275
217   210   198   188 175   240
235   266   117   173   238
207 209   236 248 176   177
279   278   261
118   215   213   271   189 199   187 178
214   186   181   179
238   260   180
234   265   276   273   184 183 182
228   122   200   213
260   217   269   275   194
263   278   102   103 264   215
273   267 237 249
277   101   256 216   231 108   209   201   193
270   220   261   274   246 252
227   247   109   274 252
100   270   224
262   116   237   202 192
238   228   110   251
115
234   252   244   242   111   126
114   191   211
272   224   112   113   231
257   216   255 205
258   220
267   132   204   131   130
273   222
251   276   253

Answer on page 51   1

See what you can pull out of your ass for this one:
Start in the opening at the top and work your way to
the bottom.

Answer on page 51

Fallen Phrases

Answer on page 51

A fallen phrase puzzle is a puzzle where all the letters have fallen down the shithole to the bottom. They got mixed up on their way down, but remain in the same crappy row.

You complete the puzzle by filling the letters into the column they fall under. You start by filling in the one-letter columns, because those clearly don't have anywhere else to go in their crap column as shown in the example below.

Also try filling in common one-, two- and three-letter words.

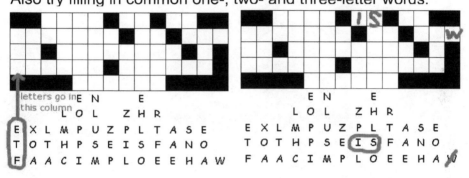

```
letters go in E  N          E
this column    L  O  L      Z  H  R
E  X  L  M  P  U  Z  P  L  T  A  S  E
T  O  T  H  P  S  E  I  S  F  A  N  O
F  A  A  C  I  M  P  L  O  E  E  H  A  W
```

```
              E  N          E
              L  O  L      Z  H  R
E  X  L  M  P  U  Z  P  L  T  A  S  E
T  O  T  H  P  S  E  I  S  F  A  N  O
F  A  A  C  I  M  P  L  O  E  E  H  A  W
```

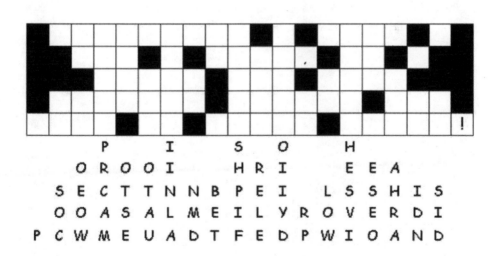

```
         P        I        S     O        H
     O  R  O  O  I        H  R  I        E  E  A
  S  E  C  T  T  N  B  P  E  I     L  S  S  H  I  S
  O  O  A  S  A  L  M  E  I  L  Y  R  O  V  E  R  D  I
P  C  W  M  E  U  A  D  T  F  E  D  P  W  I  O  A  N  D
```

Spot the 11 differences between the deuce images

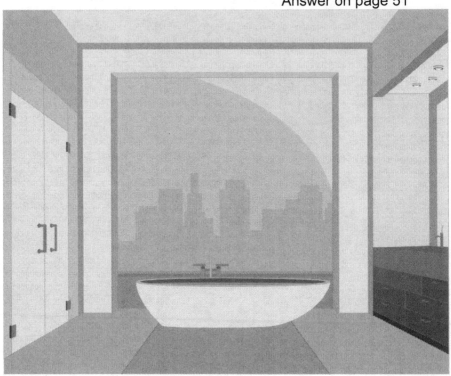

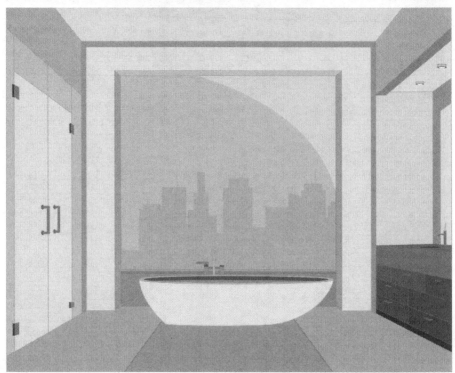

Answer on page 51

Unscramble each of the discharged words

Answer on page 51

dhcotaegl teoCslhi	
r euffttusBtl	
-doDeooosik	
tyuesuRsggt n	
d uttmBu	
oksTetrrut y	
iclonVioapwoch se	
errwausrit mcRo	
Fgebubesd ia	
Bo dysdleurob	
Kkaeer sceest	
rwSpestnee sre	
sbay nTttnu tgu	
ngfdyan Fue	
pdmRyu udp	

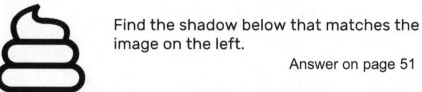

Find the shadow below that matches the image on the left.

Answer on page 51

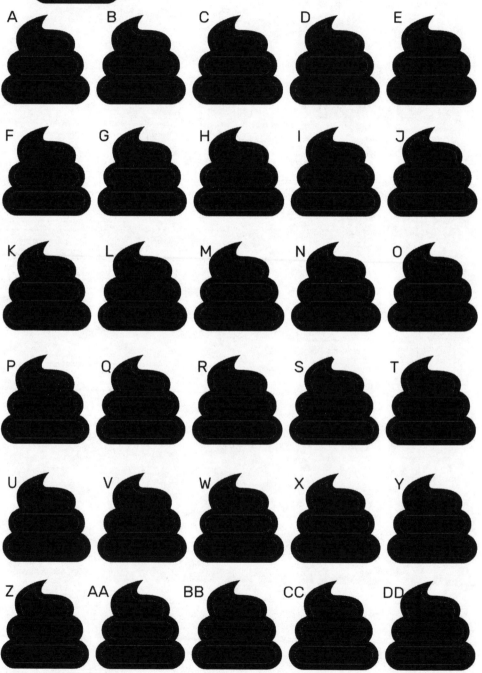

A B C D E

F G H I J

K L M N O

P Q R S T

U V W X Y

Z AA BB CC DD

Letter Tiles

Answer on page 51

Move the tiles around to make the
correct craptacular phrase.
The three letters on each tile must
stay together and in the given order in
order to finish your business.

L A T	T O	E R	O N	F .	' M	C A	O R C
W H E	K N	N E V	C A P	F S	T T	C R A	A P S
E O	I E	A P	E O	T P	E D	A B L	I R D
H J	E G G	W H A	A T	M Y	A B	R ,	N M
T I	H E M	L E	U S T	M B L	Y F	C R	R O N
O W	S O						

Search for all the fecal matter

Answer on page 52

Floaties   Dumpettes   Pooplets
Dookie   Samples   Crapsters
Business   Jujubees   Poopsters
Droppings   Dingleberries

```
M T     V Q D     A Z H     J M Z       F W I
G Q M     C C W     Q V O     P N T       C T W
  J Q Y       S H O     H I I     W C M     Q J U
    Y J R     E S Q     E C X     S X G     J X C
T     E A Y     E R C     O S Q     T Z B     O K
Q C     Q D U     B E D     G E T     E U P     Z
Q U W     O H J     U T F     F I A     L X R
  R B B     S T D     J S Q     G T P     P X T
    D F F     R K R     U P J     J A B     O Q L
O     D Q G     E K O     J A P     F O M     O F
W R     I C A     T S P     L R I     A L E     P
E M V     N J U     S Q P     X C L     N F Z
  I D P     G Q B     P T I     Q M X     T V F
    K K S     L C E     O K N     S X M     N N V
B     O X O     E T J     O Q G     A U B     B Y
D O     O M G     B J H     P R S     M E Z     E
T U H     D I V     E F S     K B T     P U D
  B M K     P Z F     R H S     Y E K     L M E
    D P A     X M Y     R G E     E Z B     E U G
D     W E A     W J I     I W N     W M H     S C
U S     F T G     Q N K     E A I     B U B     J
P T B     R T X     E X R     S L S     P L E
  V E F     N E E     G K H     D Y U     O Y D
    I V O     L S A     J R I     I Q B     D F I
      R K W     H T Q     P E P     G U R     B G
```

Find the 1 man that is different from all the other crap

Answer on page 52

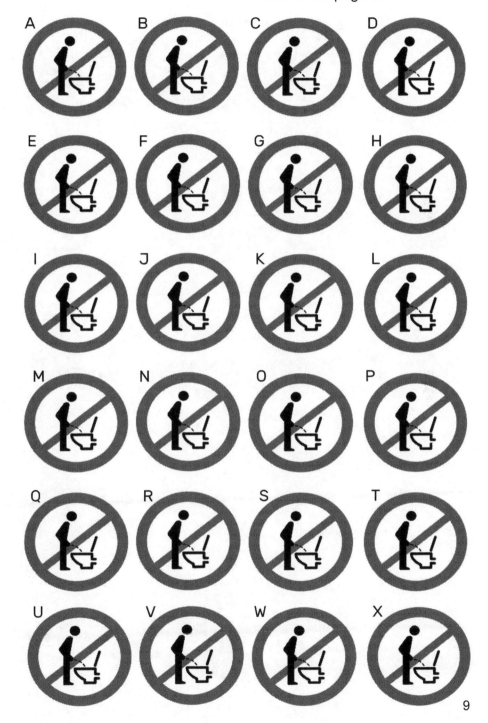

Which Poop pile Does NOT Belong?

Answer on page 52

How many fecal matter Flies can you find?

Answer on page 52

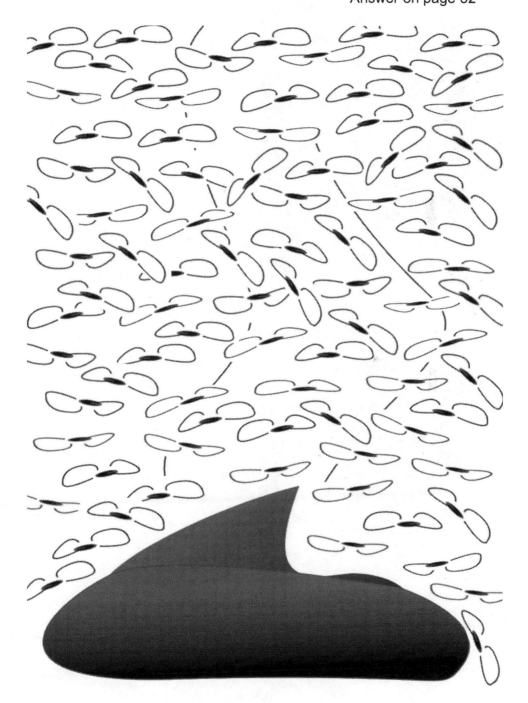

Draw the Other Half

The rules of the cryptogram puzzle:

You are given a piece of dung text where each letter is substituted with a number and you need to work out which letter in the native alphabet is being coded by the numbers you are given.

You need to use logic and knowledge of the letters and words of the language to crack the cipher and work out the crappy message by working out which number is representing each letter.

Answer on page 52

Hint: One of the words is *Poop*

A	B	C	D	E	F	G	H	I	J	K	L	M

N	O	P	Q	R	S	T	U	V	W	X	Y	Z

18 3 3 18   22 3 12 7 14   20 17 7 23   13'

6 10   1 20 21 3 17 11 13 7   12 11 23 19

3 1   22 3 12 7 14 '   15 24 13   13 25 7 10'   17 7

20   14 3 4 11 19   23 24 6 15 7 17   13 9 3.

13

Number Blocks

Answer on page 52

Try to fill the load of missing numbers.

The missing numbers are integers between 0 and 9.
The numbers in each row add up to totals to the right.
The numbers in each column add up to the totals along
the bottom. Numbers can be used more than once.
The diagonal lines also add up the totals to the right.

								32
9	0	1	3		8	4		32
4	1			4	6		3	24
5		5	1	2	4		3	28
	2	6	0	3	5	0	0	19
0	2	5	9	1		2	2	28
8	9		3	8		2	2	48
0	0	7	7	6	2	2	3	27
1	3	1	7		7	1	9	37
24	30	37	28	35	42	21	26	28

The goal of this puzzle is to figure out how to fit the numbered turd bricks into the rectangle of bricks without changing their shit shape or breaking them into smaller dunghole pieces.

Answer on page 53

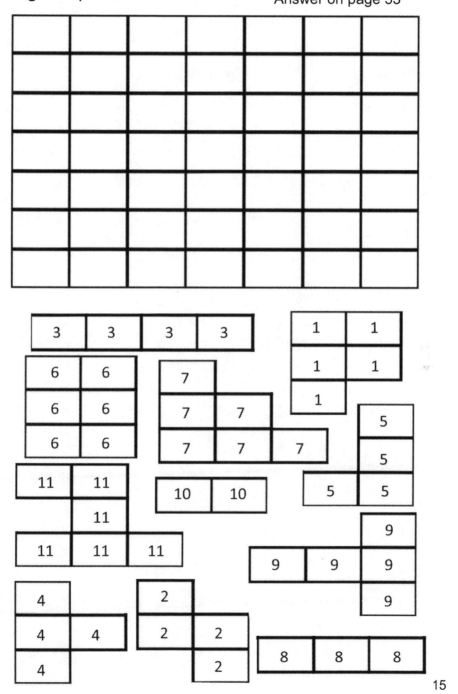

Search for the shitsicles in the toilet bowl

Waste   Shite

Deuce   Defecation

Discharge   Excrement

Shitsicles   Gobbers

Stool   Doodie

Feces

```
                                              T E
D T O N D Z S R E B B O G S V U O    R C
Z K O W J N Y K J Z Q P U G O N S    P U
K B                         F F      H E
R Z   Q A U L F N I L G K W   O Y    L D
R U   X D K Q K W F N W F A   G G    V E
G G   N U                 Q S R X    L E
X C   R Q   S E C E F   R T   E C    Z M
Y M   W E   H U B H M   R E   W M    Y M
I W   V F   I U   K L   S U   D W    D Q
Z U   R E   T K   Z N   K K   G K    O E
U K   H L   E A         E D   M L    O X
A Y   Q O   X R J G N Q X Q   Z R    D C
G P   F O   J W M R F Z Y E   Q K    I R
J C   G T                 T Z E E
T S   K S N J U A G T U A I N P O    T M
I T   S H I T S I C L E S B N A Y    U E
R A                           M N
Q X Y V D E F E C A T I O N R E Q S H T
G U L M I D I S C H A R G E M L J W N A
```

How many words can you squeeze out of:
Mississippi mud

1._____
2._____
3._____
4._____
5._____
6._____
7._____
8._____
9._____
10._____
11._____
12._____
13._____
14._____
15._____
16._____
17._____
18._____
19._____
20._____
21._____
22._____
23._____
24._____
25._____

The goal consists in finding the black boxes in each grid.

The figures given on the side and in top of the grid indicate the numbers of black boxes in the line or the column on which they are.

For example 3,3 on the left of a line indicates that there is, from left to right, a block of 3 black boxes then a block of 3 black boxes on this line. To solve a puzzle, one needs to determine which cells will be boxes and which will be empty. Determining which cells are to be left empty (called spaces) is as important as determining which to fill. Later in the solving process, the spaces help determine where a clue (continuing block of boxes and a number in the legend) may spread. Solvers usually use a dot or a cross to mark cells they are certain are spaces.
It is also important never to guess. Only cells that can be determined by logic should be filled. An example is shown here.

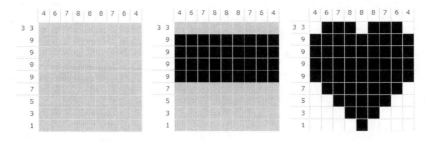

Answer on page 53

Solve the Maze: Start in the opening at top of the Poop pile and work your way to the middle.

Answer on page 53

Find the 1 image that is different from the rest

Answer on page 53

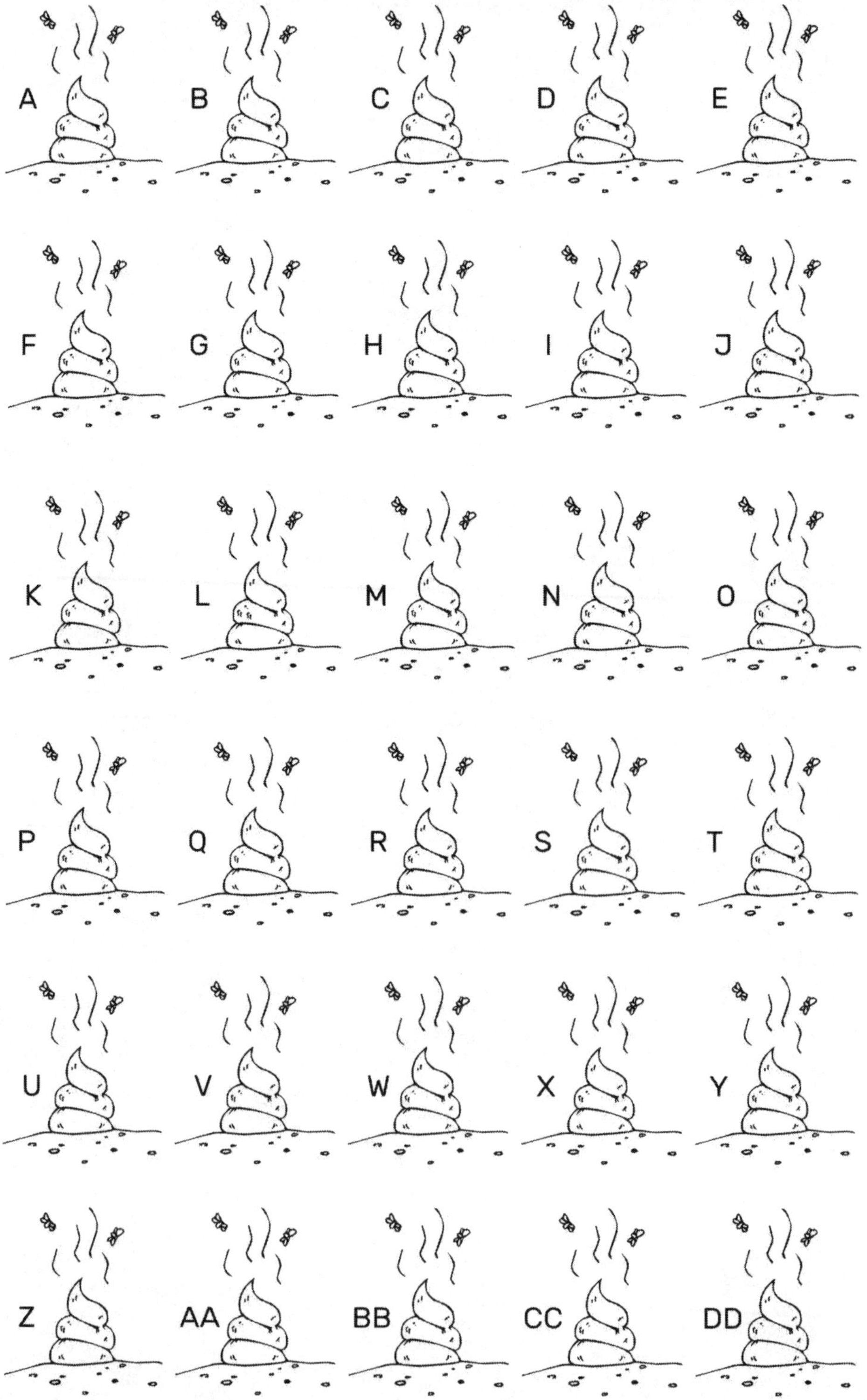

20

Connect the doodie dots from 100 to 123
Don't let the extra numbers fool you!

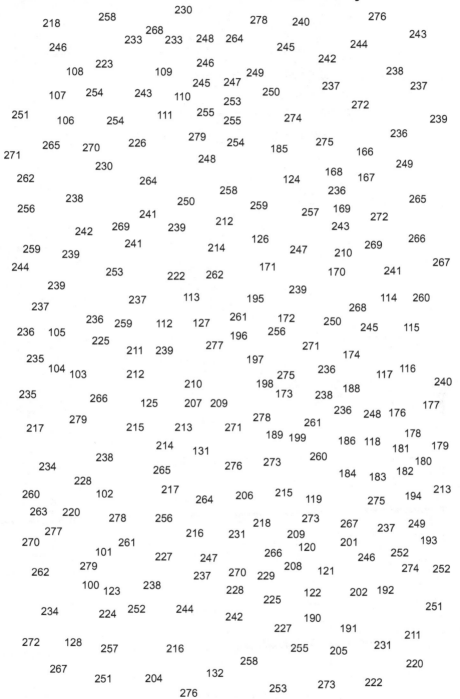

Answer on page 53

Letter Tiles

Answer on page 53

Move the tile piles around to make the correct doodoo phrase.
The three letters on each tile must stay together and in the given order.

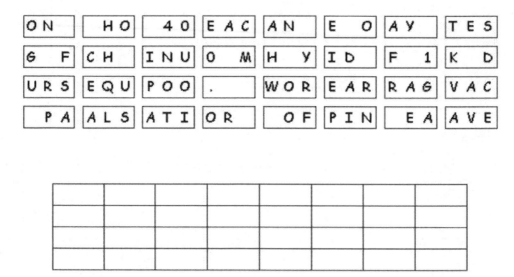

Draw each excreted image to it's corresponding square

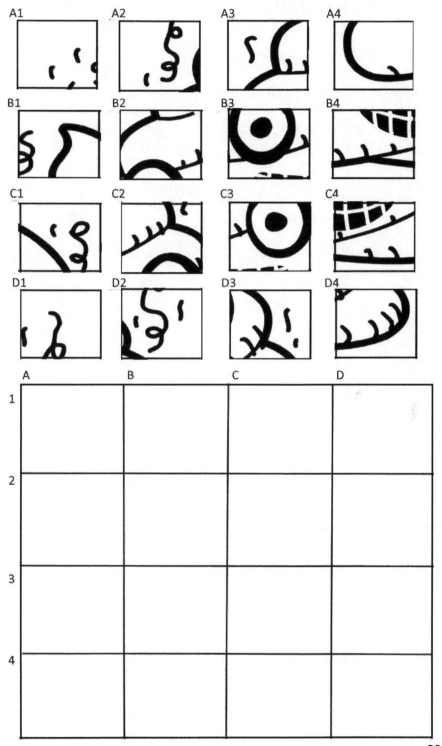

Image on page 53

Fallen Phrases

Answer on page 53

A fallen phrase puzzle is a puzzle where all the letters have fallen to the bottom. They got mixed up on their way down, but remain in the same dung heap of a row.

You complete the puzzle by filling the letters into the column they fall under. You start by filling in the one-letter columns, because those clearly don't have anywhere else to go in their column as shown in the example below.

Also try filling in common one-, two- and three-letter words.

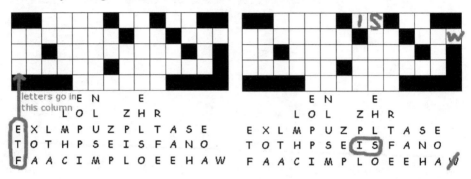

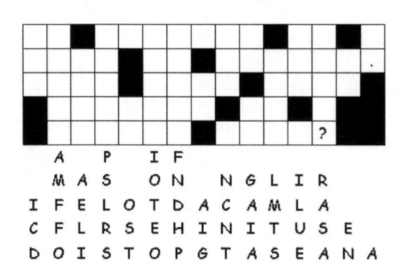

These are the rules of Sudoku   Answer on page 54

Numbers from 1 to 9 are inserted into sets that have 9 x 9 = 81
squares in whole. Every number can be used just once in every,
3x3 block, column and skid mark row.

- Every number can be used just once in the blocks of 3 x 3 = 9
  square blocks.
- Each row of 9 numbers ought to contain all digits 1 through 9
  in any order
- Every column of 9 numbers should comprise all digits 1
  through 9 in any order

One way to figure out which numbers can go in each space is to
use "process of elimination" by checking to see which other
numbers are already included within each square – since there
can be no duplication of numbers 1-9 within each square (or row
or column).

	1	4	7		2	6		5
	3	7	5		4	2	1	
		6		1		3	7	
		9		5	3			
5	4			7	8	1	2	9
7	6	8	9		1	4		
	7		3	8			4	
4	8		2		6			7
3	9	5	1		7	8	6	

Find the shadow below that matches the image on the left.

Answer on page 54

Unscramble each of the discharged words

Answer on page 54

aBsenbut t

sstas moA

po iiePpeo

Sic britkh

as sAenknal

hnkccCu abuhacs

syhsot uTt

rar donnBosgw

ooc aalbhaanCnte

moslyu vpLle

aG glnoirfirlse

p siimissuidspM

leln edBsi

kasbs Aob

rB nwotbieis

Spot the 11 differences between the poopified images

Answer on page 54

Solve the Maze: Start in the opening at the top and work your way to the anal opening

Answer on page 54

The goal consists in finding the black boxes in each grid.

The figures given on the side and in top of the grid indicate the numbers of black boxes in the line or the column on which they are.

For example 3,3 on the left of a line indicates that there is, from left to right, a block of 3 black boxes then a block of 3 black boxes on this line. To solve a puzzle, one needs to determine which cells will be boxes and which will be empty. Determining which cells are to be left empty (called spaces) is as important as determining which to fill. Later in the solving process, the spaces help determine where a clue (continuing block of boxes and a number in the legend) may spread. Solvers usually use a dot or a cross to mark cells they are certain are spaces.
It is also important never to guess. Only cells that can be determined by logic should be filled. An example is shown here.

Answer on page 54

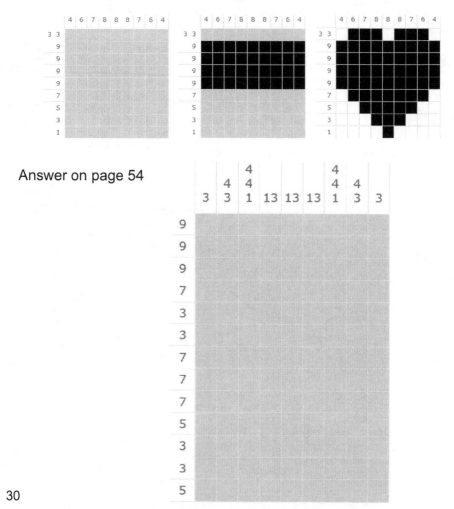

Letter Tiles

Answer on page 54

Move the tiles around to make the correct digested phrase.
The three letters on each tile must stay together and in the given order.

P O O	N E	R E	.	O N E	A P	W K W	N S	
T O	T R O	O M	A R D	T A	A B O	U T	T H E	
I N	U T	P ,	A L O	O M E	I N	I C	K Y	
H E N	Y O	R E S	W A	T H A	M E N	L K S	H I N	
U B L	T W	M O	O U '					

Search for the pooplets

Poop   Pile   Plop   Log
Shit   Turds   Dung   Dump
Crap   Doo   Load

```
                        G X W
                    U I K G V Q R R E
                  Z X R D U H C L P Y E F N
              F M A G O Q N F C T E H D Q E H K
            B Y K C O D X M D D B Y G U B K N X R
          I M J G P X T A S K V A L F N Q U V C M F
          L U J L T B P H A G P I R A G G V U R Z J
        O T P M X E     U A U Z I     I I M K W T
        C H N I F H     R E E K N     S K O D S S
    W J X F Q L E E J C M R C V I K V F S F M U R G A
    T E T H H C E A Q P O A X O K T Q Y O I L L B B B
    R T P F E H X Z B G B F U I Q B T T D T W E T I I
  Z P U C E W U W T O U J J Z G H D Z G D L M M U I D Y
  Y L R I S A G A Y Z E N Y G A K G V C U F B Z J S W I
  V U D E P X X B U L N A E Y I S V V T M B W Y L P K C
    J S O O   V V O C A U Z L M A J C W P W   B G J T
    X C Z X   V B Z B W W E J E D L Y X     U C R Q
    F G H X B     W A K H H B X S Q N G     U L U J W
    R K S Q V                         W E W B L
    Y V A H U C                       W R K S T N
      O I E I Q L Z L G Y O D R A L P P Q R G W
      Q D C E T L F L T L A R W W P L K N R V J
        T C G D K F H Q O V E Q D O M C T D O
          S X Y B H C L G R J G P O R O C H
            C G R S O N V G D X P L F
              H E F B A R I G I
              B O H
```

How many piss drops can you find?

Answer on page 55

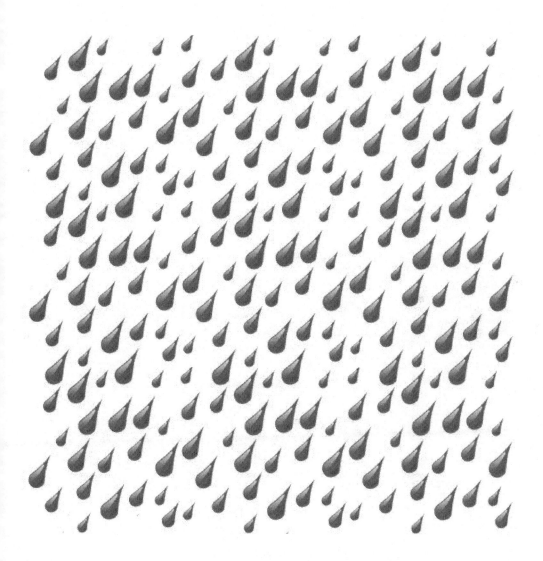

Find the 1 poopman that is different from the rest

Answer on page 55

How many words can you make out of:
Bowel Movement

1._____
2._____
3._____
4._____
5._____
6._____
7._____
8._____
9._____
10._____
11._____
12._____
13._____
14._____
15._____
16._____
17._____
18._____
19._____
20._____
21._____
22._____
23._____
24._____
25._____

Draw the Other Half

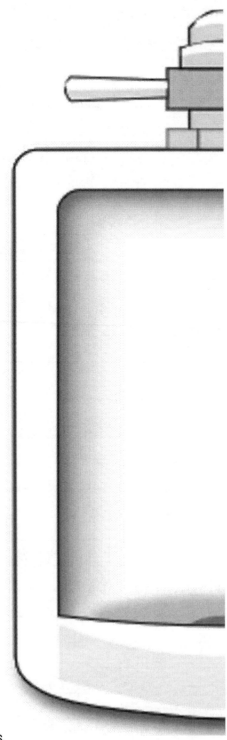

Which Sign Does NOT Belong in the space sludge?

Answer on page 55

The rules of the cryptogram puzzle:

You are given a piece of text where each letter is substituted with a number and you need to work out which letter in the native alphabet is being coded by the numbers you are given.

You need to use logic and knowledge of the letters and words of the language to crack the cipher and work out the message by working out which number is crappily representing each letter.

Answer on page 55

Hint: One of the words is *Poop*

A	B	C	D	E	F	G	H	I	J	K	L	M

N	O	P	Q	R	S	T	U	V	W	X	Y	Z

```
___ ___ ___ ___    ___ ___    ___ ___ ___ ___ ___
 5   2   7  25     26   3     15   5  25  24  25

___ ___ ___    ___ ___ ___    ___ ___ ___ ___
14   2   8     19   9   1     16   2   2  16

___ ___ ___    ___ ___ ___ ___ ___ ___ ___
22   2  24      5   2  15  25  18  25  24

___ ___ ___ ___    ___ ___ ___    ___ ___ ___ ___ ___ ___ .
11   2   1  23     14   2   8     10  25   3  26  24  25
```

38

Connect the floaties from 100 to 118
Don't let the extra numbers fool you!

278 240

218   268   233 248 264   243
   233   233   245   244
      246   242
223   122   238
238   246   243 245 247   237   237
      254   250
      119   253   272
257   255   274
251   254   279   255   239
265   254   275   236
270   226   166   124
271   248   185
262   230   264   168 167   127
               258   236
238   250   259   236   265
256   241   257 169   272
      242 269   239   212   243   126
239   241   214   171 247   269 266
259   120   210   267
244   109   253   262   121   170   110
108   222   239   241   111
237   107   239   237   195   113   112
236 259   226   261   172 250 245
236   268 225   196 256   263   131
235   211 239   277   271   174
      125 212   197   236   263
217   266   210   198 275   188 175   240
235   106   207 209   173 238   177
      100 118   278   117 236   176
123   279 105 101   213   271   189 199   114 187 178
   102   214   260 116 115   181 179
104   103   215 276   273   183 182   180
234   228   264   206   215 200 269   275 194 213
260   129 217   218 273 267 237 249
263 238   278 256   216 231 209   201   193
277   220   261   266 274 246 252
270   227 247   270 229   224   274 252
262   279   237   228   225 190 202 192
      238   251
234   224 252 244   242   227 191 128
272   130   258   255 205 231 211
267   257   216   253   220
   251 204   276 273

Find the shadow below that matches the image on the left.

Answer on page 55

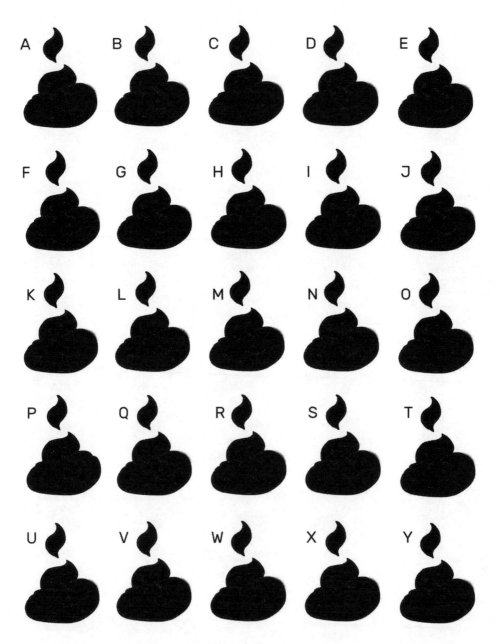

Number Blocks

Answer on page 56

Try to fill in the missing dingleberry numbers.

The missing numbers are integers between 0 and 9.
The numbers in each row add up to totals to the right.
The numbers in each column add up to the totals along
the bottom. Numbers can be used more than once.
The diagonal lines also add up the totals to the right.

								37

6	4	7	4	8	1	9		39
8	2	5	7		8		5	49
	4	1	8	9	5	6	1	37
3	7	5	2	7	5	7		42
6	7		5	9	5	3	7	50
8	1	0	5	7	7		8	45
3		5		2		3	1	27
	0	8	6		7	0	9	40
42	31	39	42	52	40	46	37	39

Letter Tiles

Answer on page 56

Move the tiles around to make the correct ass kabob phrase.
The three letters on each tile must stay together and in the given order.

T O	F A R	F E	W H Y	H A P	E L S	H I N	W I T
G O	E S S	' S	C O	M E S	, T	I T	T !
O D	O M	F R	P I N	H A T			

Numbers from 1 to 9 are inserted into sets that have 9 x 9 = 81 squares in whole. Every number can be used just once in every, 3x3 block, column and row.

- Every number can be used just once in the blocks of 3 x 3 = 9 square blocks.
- Each row of 9 numbers ought to contain all digits 1 through 9 in any order
- Every column of 9 numbers should comprise all digits 1 through 9 in any order

One way to figure out which numbers can go in each space is to use "process of elimination" by checking to see which other numbers are already included within each square – since there can be no duplication of numbers 1-9 within each square (or row or column).

5		3	9	6		7	2	1
9				7		4	3	
		2	5	1			6	
	5	9			2	1	7	
		8		4	9			6
				3		8		
2	7				1	6		9
	6	1	8					
8			4	2		3	1	

Unscramble each of the tangy butt nut words.

Answer on page 56

urirwceoar sRmt

dm nutuitBlpgs

seeagnittnwe ISe

t leorsioosTl

nikewgrsonib Ba

n pniirpdusoslDgg

beBoyo suddrl

chanksu uhCacbc

rutedTosrro p

m Muniascknenh

rwto Bsanre

gi oesdiaPrr

ouid tbBedsoy

ybeemep lSbsll

i icmasmSegrinm

Fallen Phrases

Answer on page 56

A fallen phrase puzzle is a puzzle where all the shit letters have rolled downhill. They got mixed up on their way but remain in the same dung heap of a row.

You complete the puzzle by filling the letters into the column they fall under. You start by filling in the one-letter columns, because those clearly don't have anywhere else to go in their column as shown in the example below.

Also try filling in common one-, two- and three-letter words.

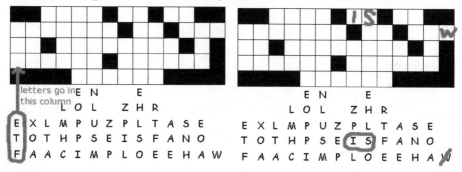

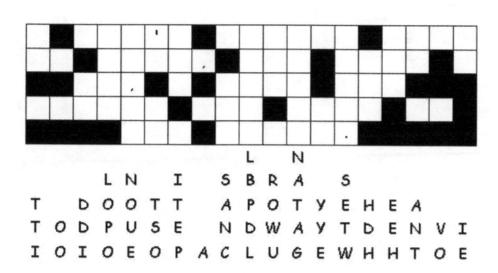

Solve the Maze: Start in the opening at the top and work your way to the opening in the center.

Answer on page 56

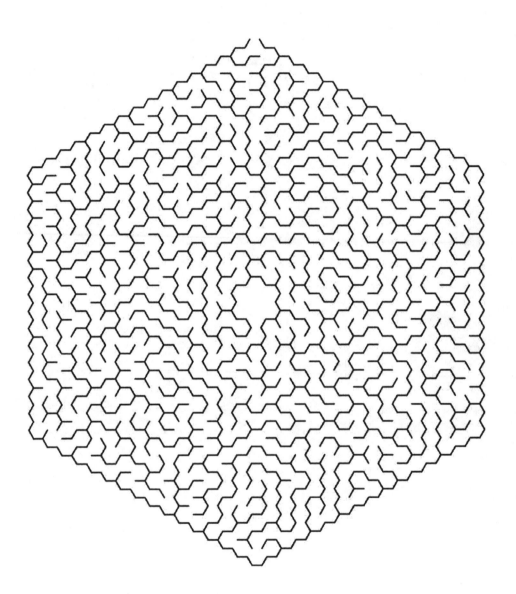

Find the 1 image that is different from the rest

Answer on page 56

A B  C  D

E  F  G  H

I  J  K  L

M  N  O  P

Q  R  S  T

U  V  W  X

Draw the image to it's corresponding square

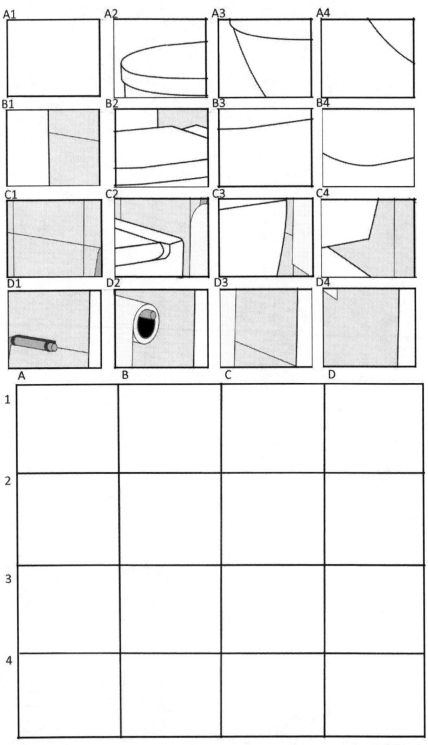

Image on page 56

Spot the 10 differences between the outhouses

Answer on page 56

Page 1

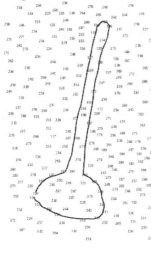

Page 2

Page 3

Sometimes I wish I was a bird, so I could fly over certain people and poop on their heads!

Page 4

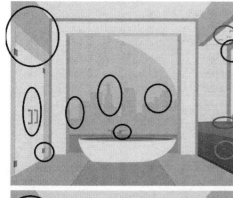

Page 5

Chocolate delights
Butt truffles
Dookie-doos
Rusty nuggets
Butt mud
Turkey trots
Volcanic whoopies
Rectum warriors
Fudge babies
Body boulders
Keester cakes
Sewer serpents
Tangy butt nuts
Fanny fudge
Rump puddy

Page 6

S

Page 7

Whenever a bird craps on my car, I eat a plate of scrambled eggs on my front porch just to let them know what I'm capable of.

Page 8

Page 9

Page 10

Page 11

No Poop Stench

Page 13

Poop jokes aren't my favorite kind of jokes, but they're a solid number two.

Page 14

3	9	0	1	3	4	8	4	32
4	1	4	0	4	6	2	3	24
5	4	5	1	2	4	4	3	28
3	2	6	0	3	5	0	0	19
0	2	5	9	1	7	2	2	28
8	9	9	3	8	7	2	2	48
0	0	7	7	6	2	2	3	27
1	3	1	7	8	7	1	9	37
24	30	37	28	35	42	21	26	28

32

86 Flies

Page 15

1	1	5	7	8	8	8
1	1	5	7	7	10	10
1	5	5	7	7	7	9
3	3	3	3	9	9	9
6	6	4	11	11	2	9
6	6	4	4	11	2	2
6	6	4	11	11	11	2

Page 16

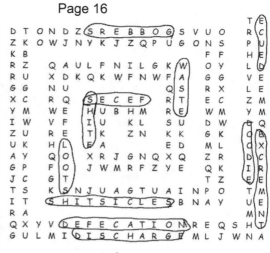

Page 18

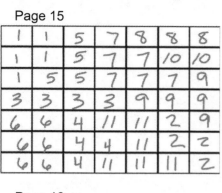

Page 19

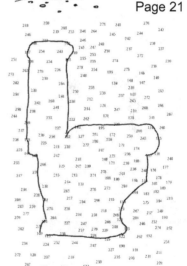

Page 20

L

Page 21

Page 22

Pooping for an average of 10
minutes each work day equals
40 hours of paid vacation each year.

Page 24

If pooping is a call of nature.
Does that mean farting is a missed call?

Page 23

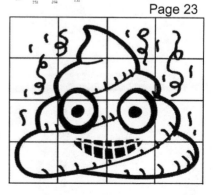

Page 25

8	1	4	7	3	2	6	9	5
9	3	7	5	6	4	2	1	8
2	5	6	8	1	9	3	7	4
1	2	9	4	5	3	7	8	6
5	4	3	6	7	8	1	2	9
7	6	8	9	2	1	4	5	3
6	7	2	3	8	5	9	4	1
4	8	1	2	9	6	5	3	7
3	9	5	1	4	7	8	6	2

Page 26

Page 27

Butt beans
Ass atoms
Poopie pie
Shit brick
Anal snakes
Chubacca chunks
Tushy tots
Brown dragons
Chocolate banana
Lovely lumps
Gorilla fingers
Mississippi mud
Blind eels
Ass kabob
Brownie bits

Page 28

Page 29

Page 30

Page 31

That awkward moment when
you think you're alone in a public
restroom about to poop,
then someone walks in.

Page32

Page33   225 Drops

Page 34

Page 38

Home is where you can poop for however long you desire.

Page 39

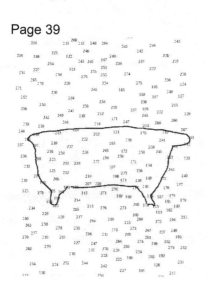

Page 37

Only Baby

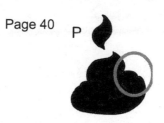

Page 40   P

Page 41

6	4	7	4	8	1	9	0	39
8	2	5	7	5	8	9	5	49
3	4	1	8	9	5	6	1	37
3	7	5	2	7	5	7	6	42
6	7	8	5	9	5	3	7	50
8	1	0	5	7	7	9	8	45
3	6	5	5	2	2	3	1	27
5	0	8	6	5	7	0	9	40
42	31	39	42	52	40	46	37	39

37

Page 42

Happiness comes from within, that's why it feels good to fart!

Page 43

5	8	3	9	6	4	7	2	1
9	1	6	2	7	8	4	3	5
7	4	2	5	1	3	9	6	8
4	5	9	6	8	2	1	7	3
1	3	8	7	4	9	2	5	6
6	2	7	1	3	5	8	9	4
2	7	4	3	5	1	6	8	9
3	6	1	8	9	7	5	4	2
8	9	5	4	2	6	3	1	7

Page 44

Rectum warriors
Butt dumplings
Intestine Sewage
Tootsie rolls
Baking brownies
Dingus dropplings
Body boulders
Chubacca chunks
Turd troopers
Mean munchkins
Brown tears
Prairie dogs
Booty buddies
Smelly pebbles
Screaming mimis

Page 45

I don't always have to poop, but when I do, I clog the toilet and need to use spray.

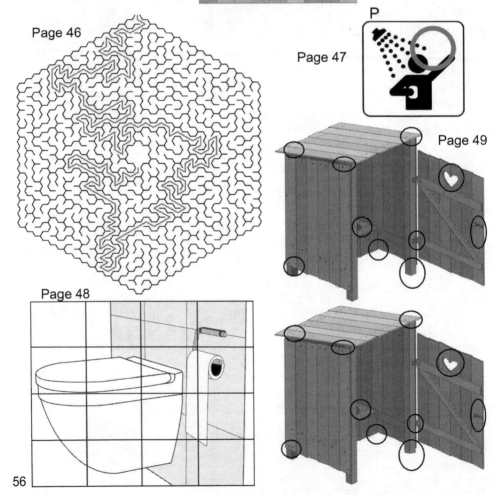

Page 46

Page 47

Page 48

Page 49

Check out these other items by the Author:

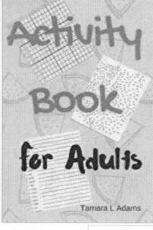

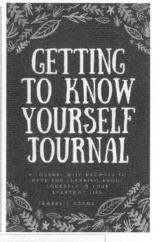

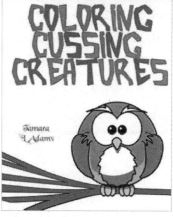

Books by Tamara L Adams

Mood Tracker Planner
Defiant (YA Dystopian Novel Series)
Art Up This Journal #1 and #2 Series
Backstabbing Bitches: Adult Activities
Puptivities: Adult Activities
Cativities: Adult Activities
Christmas Activities: Adult Activity Book/Bucket List
Activititties: Adult Activities
I Hate My Boss: Adult Activities
Activity Book for Adults
Activity Book You Never Knew You Wanted But Can't Live Without
Activity Book You need to Buy Before You Die
Fuck This Shit: Vulgar Activities
What an Asshole: Vulgar Activities
Fuck I'm Bored #1 and #2 Series : Adult Activity Book
I'm Still Fucking Bored: Adult Activity Book
The Activity Book That Will Transform Your Life
Activities to do while you number two
Unmotivated Coloring Quotes
Angry Coloring
Coloring Happy Quotes
Guided Bullet/Dot Planner
Coloring Cocktails
Cussing Creatures Color
100, 76 and 51 Quote Inspired Journal Prompts Series
Unlocking Happiness Planner
Cleaning and Organizing Planner
Daily Fitness Planner
Bloggers Daily Planner
Bloggers Daily Planner w margins
Writers Daily Planner
Busy Mothers Planner
Where's Woody Coloring Book
99 Writing Prompts
Deciding Destiny Series: Christy, Matt, Joe or Linsday
Rich Stryker Sreies: Julie's Last Hope/Tom's Final Justice
Unlocking Happiness
Getting to Know Yourself Journal and #2 Series
Timmy and the Dragon Children's Picture Book
Jacob and Ronnie the Robot Blast off to the Moon

Don't
Forget
To
Leave
A
Review
On
This
Book!

It's A
Huge
Help!

Check
Out
These
Other
Titles
By
The
Author

Thanks for your purchase!!

Please leave a review! I would be grateful.

Contact me to get a free printable PDF of Activities here at:

http://www.tamaraladamsauthor.com/free-printable-activity-book-pdf/

Tamaraadamsauthor@gmail.com

Thank you for your support and have a great day!

You can contact me at

http://www.amazon.com/T.L.-Adams/e/B00YSROGC4

Tammy@tamaraladamsauthor.com

https://www.pinterest.com/TamaraLAdamsAuthor/

https://twitter.com/TamaraLAdams

https://www.facebook.com/TamaraLAdamsAuthor/

https://www.youtube.com/user/tamaraladams

https://www.instagram.com/tamaraladamsauthor/

http://www.tamaraladamsauthor.com

All Cartoon Drawings are from https://publicdomainvectors.org

Made in the USA
Columbia, SC
26 December 2021